Living a Happy Life with a Special-Needs Child

Living a Happy Life with a Special-Needs Child

A Parent's Perspective

Volume I

Robin Williams Evans

ISBN-13: 9780989908900
ISBN-10: 0989908909
Library of Congress Control Number: 2017900164
A Pastor's Place, Silver Spring, MD

Foreword

No test or temptation that comes your way is beyond the course of what others have had to face. All you need to remember is that God will never let you down; he'll never let you be pushed past your limit; he'll always be there to help you come through it.

—1 Corinthians 10:13 (MSG)

The care of children is a unique and special calling. However, to love and guide a child with special needs is a divine calling given to a chosen few. Each and every life is precious. Planning for and bringing a new life into this world is a wonderful experience. Time spent watching the miracle of love develop and blossom from a microdot into a tiny being with hands and feet, a heartbeat, and even a gentle kick has delighted expectant parents since the beginning of time. No one is ever prepared for anything other than a full-term, healthy baby.

Yet I have spent a career preparing, rehearsing, and availing myself along with my neonatal colleagues to respond to the unexpected twists and turns that will occur in 12 percent of pregnancies in the United States and more than half of pregnancies globally.

We have been anointed to intercede on behalf of these tiny precious lives and to guide their starry-eyed parents through the shocking minefield of the neonatal intensive care unit, across the widening chasm of confusion, doubt, and anger that is channeled toward care providers, spouses, significant others, and, yes, even God. Much like Alice in Wonderland, suddenly the parents feel tossed through a rabbit hole—falling, falling, falling. Hearing people and watching mouths move while struggling to comprehend what is said, what it all means in the short and long term, and what the reason is for this utter chaos. The parents guiltily grieve the birth they did not get, the long-awaited healthy, happy, full-term little one, even though the precious child is in their presence. Once they can emerge from the land of expectations and return to the land of the present, they can get on with the business of caring for God's most precious gift—a child with special needs who will give back such incredible love, the parents cannot imagine how they missed out on it.

It is at this time that parents begin to feel the healing and understand a portion of the magnitude of their divine calling. It is at this time they begin to realize their role but long for a guide to help shorten the long fall into the pit of despair. This book will equip parents of children with special needs for the upcoming journey—a journey reminiscent of the children of Israel as they roamed in the wilderness, initially looking back with longing before gradually reconnecting with their divine helper and ultimately learning to look forward with expectation for the coming of new beginnings. For parents of children with special needs, these new beginnings will be an absolute privilege to experience. This book serves as a guide that will help these loving parents to grieve, forgive, and be revived as they continue to move forward.

This lovingly written first book is an invaluable guide to take parents from blissful ignorance through the embattled war field of multiple hospitalizations, subspecialists, insurance denials, and clueless family and friends to a prepared place that sets up families to soar to higher heights, blazing through and prepared for the unknown frontiers ahead of them. This book gives much-needed day-to-day and week-to-week survival information that will help restore order to chaotic lives, allowing the natural movement of love to so overflow the family that it can joyfully return to the give and take that is necessary to parent any child. This book is fortified with the "how to's" of walking upright and accepting the divine calling that belongs only to parents of children with special needs.

Then I heard the voice of the Lord saying, "Whom shall I send?
And who will go for us?"
And I said, "Here am I. Send me!"

—Isaiah 6:8 (NIV)

Deborah A. Hoy, MD, MDiv
Assistant pastor, Beloved Community Church
Associate professor of clinical pediatrics, Georgetown University Hospital
Attending neonatologist

Acknowledgments

THERE ARE so many people who have contributed to this book merely by being a part of my family's lives. I am grateful to the individuals who were on Wyatt's medical team in the early years. This critical group kept him breathing and eventually thriving. I am in awe of the incredibly talented and gifted group of therapists from Montgomery County Infants and Toddlers Program who worked diligently with Wyatt to help him recover some of his abilities that were lost during the birthing process. I would also like to acknowledge The Arc Montgomery County, specifically the Children's Services division, for its service to our family. This organization provides day care with a staff of nurses to medically fragile children. I have to credit the nurse navigator from the hospital where Wyatt was born for telling us about The Arc.

On a more personal note, I would like to thank my awesome friends, JoyLove sisters, phenomenal mentors, and loving family for encouraging me to write this book. I also need to extend an extra special thanks to the Honorable Lia Martin and to my pastor, Reverend Dr. Michael Bledsoe, for taking time out of their busy schedules to edit my manuscript and provide such wonderful, insightful, and heartfelt feedback. I would like to send an additional thank-you to the Reverend Dr. Deborah Hoy for considering and ultimately writing the foreword for me. You were part of the early team of medical warriors who kept Wyatt alive. My in-laws, Warren and Nellie Evans, were with us at the beginning and all the way through, supporting us in every possible way. Thank you for everything. Lastly, I would like to thank my loving husband, co-laborer, encourager, lover, lifesaver, and confidant. You have helped me to blossom into the woman God has intended me to be. Thank you with all of my heart.

Preface

THE WHOLE PURPOSE of this book is to educate families of special-needs children about how to live genuinely happy lives. When you know what to anticipate and how to possibly handle different scenarios, stress can be minimized, and happiness can set up permanent residence. The upcoming chapters contain personal stories and recommendations on how to maneuver within the special-needs world to find peace for your family. I encourage all readers to make decisions wisely, and only take my advice if it works for your situation.

My husband and I are proud parents of a beautiful boy named Wyatt. He has been diagnosed with cerebral palsy. He is nonverbal, in a wheelchair, wears hearing aids, has cortical visual impairment, feeds through a G-tube, is epileptic, and has asthma. Welcome to life's boot camp! There is actually a wonderful community of people out there who are ready to embrace you.

It's incredibly easy to get lost while navigating the complicated world of hospital staff, medical jargon, specialists, therapists, and medical-insurance claims, all while trying to find a place to exist among the madness. Wayne and I were lost in the craziness for a while and became strangers to each other, so I decided to write this book to help others avoid being sucked into the vortex. It's not a fun place to exist for anybody, including your child, so make it a priority to be a lifetime learner when it comes to navigating life with your special child.

Wayne and I have persisted at carving out a lifestyle that meets our family's needs, which allows for fun time with friends (and especially other families with special-needs children) and thriving relationships with our son's caregiving team. This book will walk you through the agonizing beginning of our journey up to when our son turned three. We live in Maryland, so some of my resource suggestions will be for this state; however, I do provide recommendations on how to discover resources in your state. I sincerely hope that our journey can inspire you on yours.

Contents

Foreword · · · · v
Acknowledgments · · · · xi
Preface · · · · xiii

Chapter 1 Our Story: A Road Map out of the NICU with Your Sanity and Health Intact · · · · 1
Chapter 2 Appointments, Appointments, Appointments · · · · 11
Chapter 3 Hospital Stays · · · · 17
Chapter 4 Medical Insurance, Prescription-Drug Insurance, Equipment, and Medical Supplies · · · · 22
Chapter 5 Services and Programs: Your Child's Team · · · · 28
Chapter 6 Childcare · · · · 33
Chapter 7 Post-traumatic Growth and Your Future · · · · 37

Works Cited · · · · 45
Further Reading · · · · 47
Resources · · · · 51
About the Author · · · · 59

CHAPTER 1

Our Story: A Road Map out of the NICU with Your Sanity and Health Intact

Wayne and I had a great pregnancy with only a few wrinkles. I was over thirty-five when I got pregnant, so the medical establishment automatically categorized me as having a high-risk pregnancy. My awful family medical history manifested in a diagnosis of pregnancy-induced hypertension and gestational diabetes. Due to these diagnoses I was in the OB/GYN's office often, but all of the issues were easily managed with a little medication and a healthy diet. We enjoyed the pregnancy and couldn't wait to meet our son.

On April 3, 2007, I went into labor. With great anticipation and excitement, Wayne and I made our way to the hospital. I was fully dilated upon arrival, so it wasn't long before I was wheeled into the delivery room. In between contractions, Wayne and I joked, laughed, and took pictures when the nurses weren't directing me to push. After approximately two hours of pushing, the mood in the room changed. Wyatt's heartbeat was no longer registering on the monitor. The doctors tried stimulating him while he was still in my womb—without success. At that point I was starting to panic. The last thing I remembered is being rolled down the hallway, on my way to having an emergency caesarian.

"Robin, Robin," the doctor called as I lazily opened my eyes. I looked around and saw my OB/GYN to my right and my husband to my left with a tear-stained face. The doctor began talking again.

"The baby isn't doing well."

I sat straight up in the bed and blurted, "What's wrong with him?"

The doctor continued, "He was deprived of oxygen for seventeen minutes, so he's not doing well."

I was in a daze as uncertainty and fear washed over me. The nurses wheeled me down to the NICU to see Wyatt before they whisked him away to another hospital for a cooling procedure in order to minimize further brain swelling. I had my husband take pictures of Wyatt because I genuinely thought this would be the last time I would ever see him.

Wayne and I had been expecting a healthy, mentally and physically intact child like everyone else who goes to a hospital to deliver their baby. Instead, we encountered a situation for which we were fully unprepared. We gave birth to a *special-needs* child. If you're not entirely familiar with this term, it basically means a person with a mental, emotional, or physical disability who may require an adaptive environment in an educational, day care, or medical environment. Despite my personal medical issues, Wyatt had been tracking excellently during my numerous doctor visits. You too may have had a typical pregnancy, and an emergency surfaced just before, during, or after birth. Or you may have been fully aware that you were about to have a special-needs child due to a diagnosis during pregnancy. The overarching theme for all experiences involving a special-needs child is the unknown path that lies ahead. This path has the power to lead a family into the wilderness, leaving them lost and disoriented, never to be reunited again if the process and experiences aren't managed well. The method of managing will vary from family to family; later chapters will go into much more detail about this.

The beginning of your child's life was most likely spent in the neonatal intensive care unit (NICU). Due to the way hospital guidelines are established, all babies are tested and measured against various standards that include hearing and vision. I believe Wyatt failed them all. He was in the NICU for almost six weeks at two different hospitals.

At the one where he was born and later returned after the emergency procedure, all we heard was that he would not hit any milestone. This was emotionally debilitating and quite unhelpful at that stage. I theoretically understood the need for the medical staff to educate us on what Wyatt's deficiencies would be so that we could plan ahead, but it felt like body blows each day Wayne and I showed up to bond with our newborn. It would be incredibly helpful if hospital staff could care for NICU families more proactively and holistically by factoring in emotional care while pouring bad news upon them. Some hospitals currently have great emotionally available social workers who do help families through trying times, but our experience wasn't consistent between the two hospitals. Perhaps consistency among institutions might get there, but special-needs families can't wait on the cavalry to come in and save the day. We have to proactively shape our new realities.

About a week or so before Wyatt was discharged from the NICU, Wayne and I decided we could no longer take any bad news about our son's situation. The information just wasn't helpful anymore, and most likely we wouldn't retain it because of our hyperstressed emotional state. We asked for a meeting with Wyatt's team of caregivers. We met with the attending physician, the charge nurse, the nurse navigator (the person responsible for discharging families with home-care equipment and services), and the social worker. My husband proceeded to lead the meeting and instructed everyone to stop focusing on Wyatt's inabilities and to concentrate on his capabilities. The staff members were shocked because they had never had this type of meeting with parents, but apparently they were positively affected because the doom-and-gloom reporting stopped.

It is up to you to begin crafting your new reality, especially in the very beginning. Here are some recommendations.

Robin's Recommendations

Take care of yourself at all times. I know this sound selfish and counterproductive because we have been taught always to put our children first, especially medically fragile ones, but having a healthy body and emotional stability are half the battle in the beginning. As I think back to Wyatt's stay in the NICU, I was sleep-deprived and didn't eat well because I was always running back and forth to the hospital for a month and a half. I was still on maternity leave, so I would spend entire days from morning until night by Wyatt's bedside. My husband would stop by the hospital after work for some Daddy-baby bonding time. I was also highly stressed and overwhelmed by all of the negative medical information I would receive upon my arrival at the NICU unit and sometimes at home, where I would get phone calls from the hospital if Wyatt had had significant episodes after I left.

Taking care of yourself can come in many forms. At the beginning of the journey, your creativity might be shot because you're just trying to survive, so I will provide a few basic tips that have worked for our family.

The most primary way to take care of yourself is by eating well. Please do not skip meals, either. I am not defining "eating well" as complicated, fancy, and expensive meals. Eating well means supplying your body with fuel it can actually use for energy, not fuel that merely tastes good and has very little nutritional value. When we are on the run, fast reigns supreme, so we may find ourselves frequenting fast-food restaurants. I know these types of places are adding more nutritional items to their menus, but often we end up overlooking them and going for the comfort food. When we make wrong food selections, our bodies spend more time digesting than they do giving us energy. This could be why we are constantly tired.

We also are doing our minds a disservice because the poor fuel selection won't make us as mentally sharp as we should be when interacting with hospital staff or other special-needs professionals. Think about it this way: if your car requires a high grade of gasoline and you continue to give it a low grade, you'll begin to notice performance issues with your vehicle. If you let it go on too long, you may start to cause significant damage to the internal workings of your vehicle. Our bodies can be viewed in the exact same light. If you feed yourself poorly, you will respond poorly and could face medical issues of your own if you continue too long on this path.

A second way of taking care of yourself is by getting a decent amount of sleep. This feat may seem impossible if your child is currently in the hospital or at home on an assortment of machines that are going off throughout the night—or if you're just too stressed. According to the National Sleep Foundation, healthy adults need between seven and eight hours of sleep each night. The Foundation also reports that the exact amount of sleep needed for optimum performance varies from person to person. I recommend shooting for seven to eight hours of shut-eye, but if that is impossible, get what you can for now. It is also important for you to release emotionally before you close your eyes to get the most restful sleep. If your subconscious mind continues to grapple with a problem during sleep, you will awake tired and agitated.

There are so many ways to release the issues of the day emotionally, but one method that has worked for us is to keep a notepad or journal by the bed. If there are tasks you are worried about forgetting to do, write them down on the pad. This way you can consult it the next morning to remind yourself of what needs to be done. You can also use the pad or journal as a source of release by writing about the day and frustrations. It is good to go back and read what you have written over the months to see how much you've grown on this journey.

Another action I highly recommend doing before going to sleep is visualizing what went wrong that day as going right. Here is your opportunity to create an ideal day. If the doctor gave you horrible news about your child's health, visualize him or her giving your child a clean bill of health. If your child is still in the hospital, visualize him or her being discharged. You may think this is hokey, but the body and mind are intricately synced with each other. If you continuously think negative thoughts, your mind sends your body these messages, which are processed in a variety of ways. Continuous negative thinking could manifest in the body as temporary or chronic diseases that will add another level of stress to your currently chaotic world. If you're interested in reading further on the mind body connection, I highly recommend Norman Cousin's *Anatomy of an Illness* and *The Biology of Hope and Healing Power of the Human Spirit*, as well as *The Secret* by Rhonda Byrne.

A third way to take care of yourself is not to forget about your significant other. When you fly on autopilot during these tumultuous times and fail to tap into your partner for strength, you are doing yourself a disservice. In the short term, you are speeding up your self-destructive pattern, and in the long-term you are fast-tracking yourself to divorce court. The divorce rate among couples with special-needs children is higher than the general population, so you have to work extra hard to keep your marriage in a good place.

It is incredibly easy to get lost in the stuff that engulfs parents of special-needs children, so you must be deliberate about pulling yourself out of the daily grind. When you are in crisis mode for long periods, it is very tough to do, and often it doesn't even cross your mind to talk to your spouse about things outside of the needs of your child. If you stay in this mode too long, you will forget what attracted you to each other in the first place. Try grabbing a bite to eat with each other every now and then, even at a hospital cafeteria if necessary. This time alone will allow you to anchor yourselves with each other again. Wayne and I found a great restaurant that was within walking distance of the hospital, and we would have a meal there every so often to brainstorm about our next steps and discuss how we were holding up emotionally.

When a partnership is working well, one is always available and strong enough to carry the other when he or she is weak. When Wayne and I got in sync with each other, our partnership functioned effortlessly. When it wasn't working, we were at each other's throats, and Wyatt was exposed to negative energy, which isn't a proper healing environment. Unfortunately, a partnership doesn't stay synced forever. It's like bathing; you've got to do it daily. You have to create some sort of protocol that nourishes it regularly. Activities we engage in that keep our partnership synced are the following:

- Turning off the television and catching up with each other through a casual conversation. I know television can be a tool you use to unwind, but turn it off for a few minutes to have a conversation with your partner. You can also use this time to brainstorm for an upcoming meeting with a doctor or therapist.
- Going out on dates. I realize childcare can be an issue because a special-needs child may require a medically trained person like a nurse. There are programs available to get this type of care, and I will go into further detail about that in a later chapter. Plan ahead, and get a babysitter or family member for just a couple of hours. An alternate date could be during the lunch hour of a work week. This way you don't have to get a babysitter. Wayne and I take this route on occasion.
- Going on vacation. This may be very difficult if not impossible to do in the early years, but once your child's medical issues stabilize, plan to take at least a two-day vacation away somewhere. Two years in a row, we were fortunate enough to go to Hawaii for about a week. This

is at least a nine-hour plane ride, depending on airline and layovers, from where we live. We took our first trip when Wyatt was three, so his medical issues had definitely stabilized. We were quite nervous about leaving him since we couldn't race home like in past times when he was having a seizure, so we dialogued a lot and reassured each other that everything was going to be OK (and it was). We left Wyatt in the very capable hands of his grandparents. The time away felt like a second honeymoon. We'd never had almost a week's worth of time just to talk to each other about us. We read, wrote, relaxed, spent time in a spa, ate great food, and did some goal setting while we were away. These trips allowed us to return refreshed and energized to reengage life with renewed vigor.

- Creating a marital vision board. For us, this is a corkboard we purchased from Target. We used pictures cut out from magazines, meaningful greeting cards, and handwritten goals scribbled on sticky notes or index cards to create a collection of goals we wanted to accomplish together in this partnership (e.g., "take a vacation in Maui," "forgive each other often," "purchase a handicap van"). We used stickpins to hold up our goals to make it easy to swap out the old ones for new ones when they were accomplished. We keep our vision board on display in the bedroom to remind us of what we are striving toward.
- Be deliberate about scheduling time to get together with friends. While on this special-needs journey, Wayne and I have been very fortunate to meet lifetime friends who also have special-needs children. We've bumped into these people at day care, at the hospital where Wyatt was born, and at doctor appointments. In the beginning, the other special-needs moms would approach me and begin conversations. I was too overwhelmed and uncomfortable with my situation ever to approach anyone. I used to avert my eyes and stare blankly ahead to avoid anyone engaging me in conversation. I did this to avoid any stupid comments someone might want to offer up about my son.

In the very beginning, Wyatt was discharged from the hospital with a nasogastric (NG) tube, which we kept using until he was about sixteen months old. This type of tube sits on the outside of the body, usually taped to a cheek, and runs through one nostril and into the stomach. It's used as a feeding device. Wyatt did not eat on his own due to an oral aversion he had developed in the NICU while intubated. I'm sure you can imagine all the stares we used to get whenever we went anywhere. Total strangers actually had the audacity to ask very personal medical questions or make offensive comments. An elderly couple even approached us while at the hospital for a doctor visit to ask what was wrong with Wyatt. I was too shocked to provide a clever and sarcastic response, so I ended up blurting out a very technical term that I knew they wouldn't understand. They shook their heads, faces riddled with pity, then left us alone. When you get this type of treatment from people all day, every day, you often decide to rarely go out if you absolutely don't have to.

Since our friends live within our special-needs world, we don't have to explain anything. There is an automatic understanding of everything. Getting together with similarly situated friends is very therapeutic and lots of fun. You can get recommendations for dentists or therapists, swap war stories, and loan one another equipment when a child outgrows it. They can also be babysitters. Hang out with this type of friend as often as you can, with and without the children. If you're not sure where to get started with regards to finding friends with special-needs children, I recommend conducting an Internet search using key words like "special-needs parent groups." To find local groups, add in your state, city, or county to the search (e.g., "special-needs parent group Los Angeles").

My fourth and final self-care suggestion is to get marriage counseling. My husband is a psychologist, and we couldn't administer our own self-healing. We were in denial about needing therapy until Wyatt was four years old. It really is imperative to seek out counseling proactively versus reactively. You don't have to be at odds with your significant other to see a therapist. You can learn about great communication techniques that significantly help out when tempers are raging. Therapy is also a great safe space to learn new insights about your partner. If you find yourself in a very bad place with your spouse, even contemplating divorce, seek counseling immediately. Do not give up on your marriage until the therapy option has been exhausted. Also, don't be timid about switching to another psychologist if you feel you're not progressing as a couple. It is imperative that both of you are connecting with the therapist.

For single parents, I also recommend therapy. Your burden is potentially greater because you might be carrying this heavy load by yourself. Therapy will be a great outlet for you as well.

Regarding prices for counseling sessions, they will vary significantly. Finances will probably be super tight because of hospitalizations, surgeries, and follow-up appointments for your child, so find a therapist with a sliding payment scale or one who takes your insurance. Also, if you work for a corporation, check your company's internal website to see if they work directly with an organization that provides these services. Your relationship and your individual well-being are worth the investment. If you don't know where to start, try the following:

1. The American Psychological Association: www.apa.org
2. Association of Black Psychologists: www.abpsi.org
3. Imago Therapy for couples: www.gettingtheloveyouwant.com
4. "Weekend to Remember" getaways in major cities, hosted throughout the year by Family Life (One of these was our first vacation away from Wyatt, and we deliberately spent it working on our marriage.): www.familylife.com
5. Your local place of worship

Success in this area is being as proactive as you possibly can when it comes to taking care of yourself. Learn from us; make changes before circumstances crush you. When we are at our worst physically and emotionally, we cease helping our children.

Rapid Review

1. Take care of yourself by eating healthy, sleeping seven to eight hours each night, and creating and maintaining an interactive relationship with your significant other.
2. Make friends with other special-needs families.
3. Get individual or couples counseling.

Relevant Reading

1. Byrne, Rhonda. *The Secret.* New York: Atria Books, Oregon: Beyond Words Publishing, 2006.
2. Cousins, Norman. *Head First: The Biology of Hope and Healing Power of the Human Spirit.* New York: Penguin Books, 1990.
3. Singer, Jonathan. *The Special Needs Parent Handbook, Critical Strategies and Practical Advice to Help You Survive and Thrive.* New Jersey: Clinton+Valley Publishing, 2012.

CHAPTER 2

Appointments, Appointments, Appointments

When Wyatt was discharged from the hospital, we were sent home with two pages' worth of appointments with countless specialists such as a neurologist, a pediatric surgeon (for consultation for a G-tube), a geneticist, a developmental pediatrician, and an ear-nose-and-throat (ENT) doctor. Luckily I was still on maternity leave, so I didn't have to coordinate my schedule with work.

Wyatt's specialists, with the exception of the developmental pediatrician, required an indefinite amount of follow-up appointments. I haphazardly handled this schedule until I realized I was at the doctor's appointments more than I was at work. This became a big problem, fast. I started dividing appointments up between Wayne and myself and realized that that wasn't working effectively, either. Wayne initially handled physical therapy (which was weekly) and ophthalmology appointments, and I handled neurology, gastrointestinal, ENT, and physical medicine. In doing so, we each developed a care niche with Wyatt, and we failed to share all details about the appointments with each other. As a side note, when you're living in an acute state of stress, it's easy to forget basic things. It became apparent after swapping physical therapy and ophthalmology appointments with Wayne that I didn't know much about Wyatt in these areas. Wayne experienced the same thing when he took Wyatt to see his other specialists. We eventually clued each other into Wyatt's vital information, but I decided not to divide up the appointments anymore. I had already started developing relationships with the specialists and had established good working rhythms, so I happily kept my group of specialists, and Wayne kept his. I also came up with a strategy that would streamline my time away from work.

Robin's Recommendations

If you have to return to work, be open with management about your circumstances. Let them know your medically fragile child will have periodic medical appointments. If at all possible, offer to make up lost time from work elsewhere in the week. If this scenario isn't ideal, have a strategy meeting with your supervisor or manager to get suggestions on how to craft a win-win situation for everyone.

Here are some ideas that may help simplify your child's follow-up schedule:

1. Create a document that includes all of your child's doctors along with their addresses, fax numbers, and telephone numbers. You can also use a contact database on your computer or smartphone. An alternate solution—if you aren't into technology—is to buy a business card holder and collect all of the doctors' cards. Record how often each specialist requests to see your child.
2. If you work full-time, I recommend scheduling your appointments either early in the morning, preferably the first time slot available, or in the last time slot in the afternoon. Some health-care providers stay late one day a week, so sometimes you can get an appointment as late as six or 6:30 p.m. Other specialists may work one Saturday a month, which would pretty much eliminate traffic headaches and most work issues. This information may not be publicly available, so ask the scheduler about flexibility.

   On a side note, if your child happens to be hospitalized at the facility where your specialist is located, maximize this time to get any outstanding tests or blood work done so you don't have to come back for that task. I know this might be the furthest thing from your mind when your precious child is lying in a hospital bed, but after enough visits, you begin to get desensitized and start thinking of ways to consolidate your efforts. Many times Wyatt's neurologist needed blood levels measured for a specific medication or video monitoring to observe any possible seizure activity.

   To get the ball rolling, ask one of the doctors or nurses during their rounds to get things that need to be done accomplished while your child is hospitalized. If a nurse happens to be drawing blood, I will ask if enough can be drawn to get phenobarbital levels for Wyatt's neurologist. Even if blood isn't scheduled to be taken, just ask if it can be done. Insurance will often treat these procedures differently than they would if you were to bring your child back after being discharged. Typically, all of these procedures will be captured under the hospital stay with only one copayment needed for being admitted. Once your child is discharged and you come back to the hospital for blood work or other tests, you could be charged an additional copayment. Check with your insurance company to be absolutely sure.

For at least the first year or so of Wyatt's life, I was letting the doctors' offices schedule me into whatever slots were available. These times would be in the late morning or in the middle of the day and would consistently destroy my work schedule. Since most of Wyatt's specialists were at one hospital, I got the brilliant idea of scheduling multiple appointments in one day to get everything over with at once. This turned out to be a horrible mess because many specialists run behind schedule, so then we ended up being crazy late to all of our other appointments. When you are either the first appointment or close to the last one for the day, you can still have a pretty full and consistent workday, which is essential if you are the parent who is providing health insurance through your employer.

3. I also recommend scheduling your appointments in clusters, so you aren't out of the office every other week or month, if it's possible. Most of Wyatt's follow-up appointments are every three months, with the exception of neurology, so I schedule them all to take place within a two-week period every three months.
4. Try to consolidate appointments when possible. For example, Wyatt used to get his flu shot from his pediatrician, but I now request it from his pulmonologist instead. We are there more often, and it will save me a trip to the pediatrician. Another example is when I needed a doctor to fill out paperwork for us to get a handicap hangtag for our van. I usually take this type of request to Wyatt's pediatrician, but

Wyatt was scheduled to see the ENT next. I brought the paperwork with me, and the doctor gladly filled it out while we were in his office.

5. If your child is fortunate enough to see most of his or her doctors at a single location (e.g., Georgetown University Hospital or Children's), take advantage of this, and request that paperwork you may need filled out for school or day care be ready for pickup while you're seeing another doctor. I do this all of the time now that Wyatt is in school. I will fax a doctor whatever form needs to be filled out, and then I will let him or her know when and where we will be. You can even request prescriptions ("scripts") for refills or equipment while visiting other doctors. I've had the information I've requested left at the front desk, or a nurse might track us down while we're in an examination room with another doctor. Coordinating paperwork and prescriptions this way will save you lots of time.
6. Get e-mail addresses from doctors or nurse practitioners. I realize many health-care practitioners don't readily give out this type of information yet, but some do. Wyatt's physical medicine nurse practitioner at Children's, Leslie Phillips, uses e-mail, and I get a ton done with her that way. She is extremely efficient and very responsive to my questions, concerns, and needs as far as getting forms filled out.

While at these follow-up appointments, don't be timid about asking questions. If you have concerns, speak your mind in a constructive way. If you feel what you're asked to do with your child isn't doing any good, ask why it is necessary and if there are alternate methods that could produce better results. A good, healthy dialogue between parents and their child's doctor is good. If you haven't been able to develop a good working relationship with a doctor for whatever reason, find a new doctor.

I also recommend doing your own research prior to the appointment on whatever you might have questions about. While reading about epilepsy, I came across information on how seizure drugs are metabolized and that they can lower critical vitamin and nutrient levels within the body. When these levels are low, it can create the opportunity for a seizure to happen. I was horrified and immediately starting running Google searches to see if I could find any other websites or studies that were publicly available. I found lots of information listing many types of over-the-counter herbal remedies, but none of the sites published dosage amounts for children. I printed off the studies and then asked Wyatt's neurologist about her thoughts on using supplements to counter the side effects of the seizure medications. She only recommended folic acid and couldn't provide dosage amounts. At that moment, I discovered that I was going to have to take Wyatt to a professional who specialized in this area.

Make it your mission to read up on your child's medical issues. You can merely type in the medical condition on any search engine and find a plethora of information. As you come across things you have questions about, print off the information, and show it to your child's doctor. If they are unable to shed any further light on the matter, ask for his or her recommendations for others who could provide more insight. You can also search the Internet to find folks by typing in the specialization and your geographic location (e.g., "homeopathic medicine Maryland").

Rapid Review

1. If your child is being followed by multiple specialists, be deliberate about developing a schedule of medical appointments. For working parents, this will potentially help you keep time out of the office to a reasonable amount. Share information from all of your appointments with others who may be helping with the care of your child. This will ensure that everyone can answer pertinent questions on the spot.
2. Get e-mail addresses whenever possible from all of your child's health-care providers.
3. If you have questions about your child's care, conduct research prior to any appointments on the subject of concern. This way you have a little knowledge on the issue and can ask specific questions.

Relevant Reading

1. Coleman, Avis. *SPECIAL NEEDS: Special Families*. IN: AuthorHouse, 2014.
2. Cooper, Contessa Louise. *Mad at the World: How to Move On and Find Peace When You're A Special Needs Parent*. MD: Contessa Louise, 2015.
3. Hernandez, Geri. *Medically Fragile Training Manual*. OK: Tate Publishing & Enterprises, LLC, 2010.

CHAPTER 3

Hospital Stays

It's never pleasant when your child has to be admitted to the hospital. Wayne and I have had plenty of experience with having to rush Wyatt to the emergency room for seizure and upper-respiratory issues. One time I even took Wyatt to a pediatrician appointment, and they wanted to call 911 with me sitting right there. Since I was so used to what Wyatt was experiencing that moment—upper-respiratory issues—I insisted I could take him myself.

Robin's Recommendations

We were in the ER so often for the first two years of Wyatt's life, we knew most of the staff. After the initial trip, it doesn't feel like a scary place anymore. The routine will become typical to the point of your being able to anticipate the process as well as what information the doctors will need. You will be navigating a ton of different personalities in a stressful environment within a short period of time, so I have some recommendations for how to prepare for these trips.

1. Pack a hospital bag for your child. Keep it stocked and out of the way in a closet until you need it. If you think you're going to forget key items, just prepare a list of things to bring, and save it as a file on your computer. Things you may want to keep in the bag include the following:
    a. Diapers and wipes (if your child needs them). If your child hasn't been admitted yet, these supplies are not readily available to you.

b. Bibs and an extra change of clothes and socks. Make sure the clothes and socks are not white. Sometimes your child might bleed when procedures are being performed, and white will immediately show everything. Also, white clothing and socks may be mistaken for hospital property, so keep things clear by bringing colorful garments.

2. A small supply of formula, if your child needs it. Again, supplies aren't readily available if feeding time comes up, and your child hasn't been given a room yet. If the staff gives you the OK to feed your child, you can feed him or her immediately because you came prepared with your own supplies. Another reason to bring small amounts of formula is to show the staff the exact brand you need. I've run across nurses who weren't familiar with what we used, and they were able to figure things out more quickly when they had something tangible in their hands to examine. Even if the hospital doesn't use the same brand, they can read the label to see what comes closest in their supply room.
3. If you are still providing breast milk to your child, make sure to bring your pump. Within the pockets of your pump, keep a writing utensil and labels. Also throw a freezer bag or ice pack into the hospital bag if you can remember before running out of the house. This will help keep your breast milk cold until your child is assigned a room. If you forget to bring a freezer bag or ice pack with you, use your labels on the bottles, and ask the staff to refrigerate the breast milk for you. I was never refused refrigeration for my milk, but come prepared just in case.
4. Prepare a list of medications and over-the-counter drugs you give your child. Make sure to include the dosages and how frequently your child takes the medications. Print out multiple copies, and keep them in the hospital bag. This is a routine question you will be asked a thousand times while you are at the hospital. You will save your voice and sanity by having lots of copies to provide. And let people know they can keep the print outs.
5. Bring the actual medications your child will need if he or she is admitted to the hospital. You most likely won't have to use your supply

because the hospital has its own pharmacy, but every now and then your child may receive a prescription that is confusing to fill. Without fail, I would get tons of questions about Wyatt's baclofen prescription. I started bringing the phone number and e-mail address of the nurse practitioner who prescribed the med so whomever had questions could speak directly to her, but in the meantime the hospital would actually allow me to administer the medication we brought from home. Since Wyatt suffers from seizures, it is incredibly important that we always have his medications with us. We are required to give him his medications at the same time every day to minimize possibly opening a threshold for a seizure. This is only a potential problem while you're waiting in the ER, or you have received a room assignment during a shift change (usually 7:00 a.m. or 7:00 p.m. in most hospitals). Once your child is admitted, medications are given like clockwork. Always ask a staff person before giving your child his or her medications.

6. Bring a few comforts from home for you and your child. For us, an ER visit is at least a four-to-five-hour adventure, and if Wyatt is admitted, the stay seems to be nothing less than three days. Many hospitals offer Wi-Fi, so make sure to bring your electronic gadgets to help pass the time and to keep in touch with your community support.

If your child is admitted and will be in the hospital for a series of days, talk over a family coverage plan with your spouse or other relatives. Wyatt is our only child, so we don't have to create any plans of care for other children. Since Wayne and I both work full-time, it is important to be able to do so and still care for our child while he is in the hospital. When Wyatt is hospitalized, we alternate spending the night with him so both of us aren't exhausted and stressed out. My in-laws will also come to town so that they will be available to stay with Wyatt throughout the day and night. This way Wayne and I can have restful nights and good workdays.

Don't allow yourself to get overwhelmed by medical jargon. Sometimes health-care professionals forget that the terms they are using aren't in our everyday vocabulary. Remind them by asking lots of questions until you understand what's going on with your child and what options you have. Just because they don't mention some options doesn't mean they aren't available to you. Do your own research by talking to family, friends, and other special-needs parents. You can also scour the Internet. Your search terms will vary greatly depending on the subject matter of interest. For example, if you are looking for discussions of what vitamin and mineral supplements work best alongside seizure medicines, your search terms can be "vitamins or mineral supplements and seizures." I also recommend typing in your child's disability with other terms you may be interested in, like "Downs syndrome and psoriasis."

Also, if you don't have any friends yet with special-needs children, you can find a ton of forums on the Internet that can be great resources for you (search for something like "Cerebral palsy support"). And be on the lookout for new friends with special-needs children to add to your circle. They will become an invaluable network for you and friends for life.

Lastly, your child may be discharged with equipment like an oxygen supply. Don't let lots of equipment overwhelm you. Wyatt's bedroom looks like a mini-hospital to this day, but that has significantly cut down our hospital runs because we have the key equipment at home. Don't worry if the various parts and pieces begin cluttering your house. Other people's perceptions should not be more important than the health and comfort of your child. If others don't understand, it is their responsibility to educate themselves. You have enough on your plate to deal with, and managing a family member or friend's emotional needs isn't one of them.

One tip I'd like to provide is to request an oxygen-concentrator machine if your doctor prescribes an oxygen tank. I discovered well after the fact that there is an oxygen-concentrator machine that doesn't require any refillable tanks. I no longer have to wait around for any type of tank. Another script will need to be written by the prescribing doctor to make this simple change. Tank-size classifications can be incredibly confusing, and you are committed to sitting at home for a block of hours every so often for the home medical-supply company to deliver new tanks and remove the empty ones. If you work full-time like I do, this can wreak havoc on your work schedule.

Rapid Review

1. Always be prepared with a fully stocked diaper bag just in case you have to make a trip to the ER. It's always tough to think of everything you will need when your child is in need of immediate medical attention.
2. If you have multiple children, create a family-coverage plan with friends or relatives in the event that your special-needs child has to be hospitalized.
3. Don't be overwhelmed by the medical jargon doctors use to describe what's going on with your child. Ask lots of questions until you fully understand.

Relevant Reading

1. Bradley, Lorna. Special Needs Parenting: From Coping to Thriving. MN: Huff Publishing Associates, 2015.
2. Kimpton, Diana. *A Special Child in the Family: Living with your sick or disabled child.* London: Sheldon Press, 2011.
3. Philo, Jolene. *Different Dream Parenting: A Practical Guide to Raising a Child with Special Needs.* MI: Discovery House Publishers, 2011.

CHAPTER 4

Medical Insurance, Prescription-Drug Insurance, Equipment, and Medical Supplies

Navigating the world of insurance can be a full-time job. I have spent countless hours trying to understand our deductibles, our out-of-pocket responsibilities, and what's covered and not covered as well as appealing things that get rejected, etc.

You mustn't let your temper or frustration get the best of you while speaking with insurance representatives. It's not their fault that things get rejected. It could be the limitation of the plan you selected or restrictions your employer has added. You must be educated about your plan's coverage and be ready to appeal rejections. Sometimes employee insurance plans come with the complimentary option to use a third-party health advocate to help you with your appeals. If you can't find evidence of this coverage on your employer's website, call the human resources department, and inquire about it. Unfortunately, since so many medical plans exist, I can't get too specific in this area. However, I still have lots of recommendations to consider as you wade through all of the red tape.

Robin's Recommendations

1. Log onto your medical or prescription-drug insurance's website, and become intimately familiar with the following:
   a. What is your deductible? The amounts could be different depending on the type of appointment and specialist. There are also deductibles for equipment. Most insurance coverage will require

a specific out-of-pocket maximum before copays are eliminated. The process will typically start all over at the beginning of the new year. Check the provider's website frequently to keep track of claims and progress toward meeting the deductible.

b. Can you go to in-network or out-of-network health-care providers or therapists? If your plan allows for out-of-network providers, how much does it pay, and how much are you responsible for paying? It has become industry standard to provide in-network physician directories on insurer websites, so make sure you find this out before accidentally meeting with an out-of-network provider. You don't want to get a huge surprise bill.

c. How many physical therapy (or any other type of therapy) sessions are included in your plan annually? How does the insurance company count the physical therapy sessions (e.g., are they considered inpatient or outpatient)? If you take your child to a hospital to see a physical therapist as an outpatient, sometimes these sessions are not counted toward your annual limit. That was the case for Wyatt on a previous insurance plan. You must definitively find out how the sessions are counted, and try not to schedule too many during the year; you don't want to pay out-of-pocket for each session over the annual limit. Depending on the therapist and facility, physical therapy sessions could cost you more than $700 per session if you go over. If too few are covered for the year, this may be something that needs to be appealed. You can work with your child's therapist to draft a letter to the insurance company. I'll speak about the appeal process in more detail a little later.

d. What type of equipment is covered (e.g., hearing aids, wheelchairs, bath chairs, ankle-foot orthotic brace), and how often can you get new ones (e.g., every three-to-five years for wheelchairs)? Equipment companies require scripts to be written by a doctor before anything can be ordered. This is pretty routine and not a big deal for doctors to do. Just be very specific about what you need written on the script (e.g., "60 mL syringes").

2. Regarding prescription drugs, transition the refills to mail order if possible. This will simplify your life tremendously. The only potential problem is initially setting everything up. Make sure not to wait until the medicine is nearly depleted before you begin setting up your mail order. This process was a huge headache for me because I couldn't get a couple of the doctors to respond in a timely manner to the mail-order pharmacy's request for information, and Wyatt had started to run out of some of his medications. When a prescription is in transition, you can't just run to the local pharmacy and get refills unless you ask the prescribing doctor to write a prescription for a few days' worth of a particular medicine. It was a big mess. So, make sure to start the process when all meds are no less than halfway consumed. I also recommend getting the doctors to prescribe three-month dosages with a couple of refills. This way you are set regarding medicine for three months at a time.
3. You have to stay organized in regard to medical supplies. Some companies are pretty good about sending orders out on a timely basis, and others aren't. I find myself calling one medical supply company monthly to make sure Wyatt's order is queued up for delivery. If I don't, I might find myself running out of something I can't buy at the grocery store. The other medical-supply company I work with offers automatic reorders every month. It's still not a perfect system; it has occasional hiccups, and sometimes a manufacturer has the needed supply on backorder.

   Such hiccups cause tremendous waves in your life, so it's important to discover any problems as early as possible. If too many problems exist with one company, fire them, and go find another one. You can easily find hundreds of medical-supply companies for non-prescription items like formula or diapers on the Internet (e.g., JRS Medical or Allegro Medical).
4. If your insurance company denies something you really need, appeal the denial. Make sure you understand the appeals process before you mail anything. Check your insurance company's website, or call their

customer-service number to get the details you need. Sometimes doctors or equipment companies will appeal on your behalf and often without your knowledge. I have received countless letters from our insurance company saying they have received an appeal and are considering the request with reasons why. These letters used to confuse the heck out of me until I began to understand the process, or sometimes someone would give me a heads-up that an appeal had been sent in on our behalf.

On occasion, the doctors or medical-supply companies might need your personal testimony regarding why a certain treatment or piece of equipment would make your child's life better. I had to provide this to Hill-Rom for the Vest. Our medical insurance initially denied this $17,000 piece of equipment that is especially essential for people who suffer from upper-respiratory issues. I wrote a testimonial that explained how the Vest would bring quality of life to Wyatt, and I found a study on the Internet that documented how children who suffered from cerebral palsy benefited from similar chest-compression machines. The appeal was approved, and we were able to get the machine for Wyatt.

Don't give up easily if your child really needs something. Some doctors might be willing to write letters to insurance companies on behalf of your child, but you have to be willing to find the energy to fight these battles. I realize this is the last thing you probably want to hear because you are fatigued and overwhelmed, but you must make the effort to do what is necessary to get critical equipment. In the long run, your child will be healthier with the proper equipment, which will contribute significantly to your happiness.

5. Equipment is expensive, and sometimes essential items aren't covered by insurance. Find an equipment-sharing program (see chapter five for more details), or make friends with other special-needs families. Equipment-sharing programs usually involve parents donating used equipment to organizations that then loan it out to other special-needs families. Unless you're wealthy, this is a critical to-do item now that

you're on this special-needs journey. I know that an insurance company not covering essential equipment for a child doesn't make sense, but that is the world we are forced to navigate.

By making friends with other families with special-needs children, you can share essential items (such as bath chairs or seating). Wayne and I have made the greatest connections with people we are certain will be lifelong friends. Although we didn't ask to be on this path in life, we wouldn't trade the opportunities we've been given to meet such wonderful people. I have a few friends now with whom I share equipment. When their children get too big for something, they give it to Wyatt. We do the same thing in return. In addition, Wyatt's physical therapist has been phenomenal in connecting us with other parents who no longer need things, and then we return the favor by giving Wyatt's old equipment to her to share with other families (like his power wheelchair). When you do good, the good comes back to you.

Rapid Review

1. Know your medical benefits and coverage in full detail. Make a point to figure out what is in-network and out-of-network before going on any appointments.
2. Elect to get mail-order refills if this is an option under your prescription-drug insurance plan. Ask your doctor for a three-month supply with at least one refill.
3. Stay organized. If your child receives supplies from a medical-supply company, keep track of the supplies so that you don't run out. You may have to call the supply company monthly to remind them to send out your order.

Relevant Reading

1. Lavin, Judith Loseff. *Special Kids Need Special Parents: A Resource for Parents of Children with Special Needs.* New York: Berkley, 2001.
2. Vujicic, Boris. *Raising the Perfectly Imperfect Child: Facing the Challenges with Strength, Courage, and Hope.* Colorado: WaterBrook, 2017.
3. Wells, Nora. *Paying the Bills: Tips for Families on Financing Health Care for Children with Special Needs.* Boston: New England SERVE, 1999.

CHAPTER 5

Services and Programs: Your Child's Team

When your child gets an official diagnosis (e.g., cerebral palsy, Down syndrome, etc.), he or she is potentially eligible to receive services through the county in which you live. On a quick side note regarding diagnoses, if you have been unsuccessful in getting doctors to see that there is a problem with your child, don't give up. Document everything (such as dates and times of when episodes happen, frequency of occurrence, what's happening, etc.), videotape your child, do your own research, and find different doctors if the ones you currently have won't listen to you.

Many states offer early-intervention programs for children with developmental delays, but the names of the services vary greatly. The state of Maryland calls it "Infants and Toddlers." To find this program in your state, please visit the Center for Parent Information and Resources website at www.parentcenterhub.org/repository/services-ei/. You will be able to navigate to your state's service offering from this page. Check to see if this program is available for free for state or county residents or if there is a fee on a sliding scale.

Wyatt's hospital proactively contacted Infants and Toddlers for us. Once you locate services for your state, check the website for how to request an evaluation. The staff will test your child to see if he or she is eligible for services often without waiting for an official diagnosis. In Maryland, this program goes to the age of five, but families with children as young as three years old can choose to transition into the public schools' special education pre-K programs. Other states' early-intervention programs end at the age of three, and children have to be reevaluated to determine next steps. Make sure to inquire about options in your area.

Wyatt was fortunate enough to work with the Montgomery County Infants and Toddlers Program in Maryland (MCITP). You may want to consider moving to a different county if yours lacks such services. This move might be a hassle, but your child might miss out on some significant services that could positively affect his or her well-being and yours. After some initial testing, Wyatt was eligible for hearing, vision, feeding, and occupational therapy and physical therapy. These services are sometimes offered for free to families, like in Maryland, and sometimes states might charge a fee on a sliding scale. Depending on your state or county service option, you can choose to have the therapies given to your child at day care or in the comfort of your own home. Since Wayne and I both work full-time, we elected to have the services at Wyatt's day care. You can also meet the provider at the day care and participate or observe the sessions. While testing your child, staff will determine how frequently your child may need a service per week or month, depending on the severity of the child's delays. Wyatt was getting vision, feeding, and occupational therapy and physical therapy twice a week each. Hearing services were once a month.

Wyatt was officially enrolled in the MCITP program when he was about four months old. He was stiff due to having spastic quadriplegia. He had zero peripheral vision and could look only to the right side. We were assigned a stellar group of therapists to whom we give much credit to for helping our child begin to regain his abilities. His physical therapist, Ginny Paleg (www.ginnypaleg.com), is amazing because she used unconventional therapies like treadmills with Wyatt to get him to take steps. She also had the foresight to put him in mini-power wheelchairs to get him used to using buttons and following commands like "stop" and "go" at nine months of age. Wyatt is able to use his power wheelchair pretty well now with consistent practice. Ginny also partnered with us to get Wyatt customized equipment for a lower cost or sometimes for free due to her connections and our willingness to let various organizations tell the story of Wyatt's progress while using their equipment. If your therapist isn't this proactive, be creative, and contact equipment manufacturers on your own. Offer a barter arrangement like free or lower-cost equipment for allowing them to feature your child using their equipment on their web page.

Robin's Recommendations

Lots of organizations give funding assistance. It's impossible to provide a complete list that offer funding and parent resources because there are so many great ones out there. Please consult the resources section at the end of the book for a list of supportive services and information.

I mentioned in chapter four that your therapist can potentially connect you with other parents they are working with who have old equipment they are willing to pass onto you. Wyatt has benefitted significantly from other parents passing along equipment. He is currently using a manual wheelchair that has been recycled. We just passed along his old power wheelchair to another family because we ordered a new one through our insurance. I also want to remind you about becoming friends with other parents of special-needs children. Within this circle of friends, you can recycle equipment that might not be covered by insurance.

Regarding legal services, this area is quite broad and can require a large time commitment. If you feel that your child has sustained a medical injury, contact a law firm, and schedule a consultation. You can find an enormous amount of firms online advertising services for specific disabilities like cerebral palsy, Erb's palsy, and so forth. Just search for your child's disability or diagnosis and the phrase "special-needs law firm."

Lawsuits might take a number of years before you actually go to trial, and sometimes settlements are offered days prior to going to court. It is good to keep up with legislation that could potentially affect the services your child receives as well as insurance coverage for equipment and programs. Two groups that do a great job of monitoring bills regarding individuals needing wheelchairs are the National Registry of Rehabilitation Technology Suppliers (www.nrrts.org) and the National Coalition for Assistive and Rehab Technology (www.ncart.us). Both groups, in association with *New Mobility Magazine*, sponsor annual conferences called CELA in the Washington, DC, area. The conferences are quite informative, and the organizers can schedule meetings with your elected officials to discuss a variety of topics.

Wayne and I were fortunate enough to participate in a few of these face-to-face meetings with our elected officials. It was exhilarating to be able to tell our story directly to the person who represents our district on Capitol Hill. I recommend conducting an online search to locate organizations that support your child's disability. Just type in the name of the disability followed by "advocacy," "legislation," or "regulations" and "US" or "United States."

Rapid Review

1. Get your child enrolled into an early-intervention program as soon as possible.
2. There are many organizations that provide funding and resources for parents of special-needs children. Make sure to check the Web sites listed in this chapter for assistance.
3. Contact a lawyer immediately for a consultation if you believe your child's diagnosis is due to a medical mistake, and keep up with state and federal legislation and regulations that could affect services and insurance coverage.

Relevant Reading

1. Crawford, Merle J. and Barbara Weber. *Early Intervention Every Day!: Embedding Activities in Daily Routines for Young Children and Their Families.* Baltimore: Brookes Publishing, 2013.
2. Kaufman, Sandra and Robert Edgerton. *Retarded Isn't Stupid, Mom!* Baltimore: Brookes Publishing, 1999.
3. Keilty, Bonnie. *The Early Intervention Guidebook for Families and Professionals: Partnering for Success.* New York: Teachers College Press, 2016.

CHAPTER 6

Childcare

Finding childcare for special-needs children, especially those with physical disabilities who need nursing, can be exceptionally difficult. We were fortunate enough to find a day care that takes medically fragile children; there is a nursing staff, and the special-needs children are integrated into a population of typically developing children. It's a fantastic place that has been our sole beacon of light since the early days of Wyatt's life. This day care is run through The Arc Montgomery County in Maryland (thearcmontgomerycounty.org). This organization was designed to serve the needs of those with intellectual and developmental disabilities and their families.

Robin's Recommendations

All fifty states and the District of Columbia have an Arc, so I recommend going to www.thearc.org to find your state's chapter. Once you're on the chapter's website, you should find local Arc chapters listed. On the local Arc websites, check under "Services" to see if they offer children's services. If they don't, you might want to consider hiring a professional childcare provider to care for your child at home. If necessary, I also recommend retaining a nursing agency to assist the childcare professional at whatever frequency it might be needed. This benefit could be a part of your medical insurance coverage. If it's not, there are many organizations that offer private nursing. Just conduct an online search for "pediatric nursing," and make sure to add your geographic location to the search query. An organization we plan to use in the near future is called Continuum Pediatric Nursing (www.Continuum-Nursing.com). They have multiple locations across the United States. I found out about them at the

Accessibility Summit, sponsored and hosted by McLean Bible Church. Also, check out nationwide pediatric-nursing care organizations like Maxim Home Care (www.maximhomecare.com), Interim Healthcare (www.interimhealthcare.com), and BrightStar Care (www.brightstarcare.com), to name a few.

If your child isn't medically fragile, then feel confident about placing him or her at a childcare center with his or her typically developing peers. It may be awkward in the beginning when parents and kids are getting used to your child, especially if his or her disability is physical, but the benefits definitely outweigh the discomfort others might feel in the beginning.

Our family experienced this exact scenario when Wyatt was four. He had started out at a day care center for only medically fragile children and their siblings, but the center was forced to move because the county wanted its facility back. We ended up joining another day care that was also a part of The Arc Montgomery County, but it was for typically developing children.

At the first day care, there had been twenty-five families and only six to eight kids in each classroom (except the baby room, where there were only six); now there were more than 130 families and upward of twenty-two kids per classroom. I was overwhelmed and didn't know what to expect. Wyatt stood out like a sore thumb because he was the only kid in his class who was in a wheelchair. Kids and parents alike had questions, especially when the nurse came in to feed Wyatt via his G-tube. I didn't mind answering these questions because the other children and parents were just interested in learning about my child rather than making assumptions and casting judgment. Earlier in Wyatt's life, I would bristle when total strangers asked medical questions because it felt intrusive. In the day-care setting, I felt safe and affirmed. I too was guilty of making my own assumptions about people and learned that folks just didn't know or might have been too embarrassed to ask.

Wyatt also thrives in this environment. He's very social, and I think the setting encourages him to do more to keep up with his friends. The kids compete to push Wyatt around in his wheelchair while on the playground. He also gets invited to his typically developing peers' birthday parties. Kids usually don't care about disabilities, but unfortunately their ill-informed parents teach them incorrectly about our community. By blending our kids, parents and their children get great life lessons about the disabled community, and we learn a great deal, too.

If you have the option of using extended family to care for your child, take full advantage of the opportunity. Family support, even though it may be infrequent, is absolutely critical. I realize that this option isn't available for everyone. If not, that's OK. You can tap into your network of friends to help out with childcare. Just remember, you still might need to hire a nursing agency to come periodically if your child is medically fragile.

Family and friends will provide you with opportunities to get uninterrupted sleep, to get extra work done, or to go out to dinner or to a movie. They also can provide emotional support. Wayne's parents have been a huge blessing to us. They live about seven hours away, but they come regularly to give us time to ourselves. It's essential to have your own time to replenish your reserves.

There is another childcare service I would like to share with you: an organization called Jill's House (jillshouse.org). They provide respites for children with intellectual disabilities and their families in the greater Washington, DC, area. Their goal is to ensure that parents and caregivers get real breaks, so their program includes overnight stays for the children. This remarkable organization gives parents time in their schedules to focus on their marriages or to spend with their other typically developing children. Jill's House cares for children from ages six through seventeen, so Wyatt is now able to take full advantage of this fantastic program. I encourage you to conduct searches online to find similar organizations in your area. My suggestions for search terms include "respite care," "special-needs child," and your state of residence. Please see the resources section at the end of the book for suggestions.

Rapid Review

1. If you are in need of childcare, go to www.thearc.org. This organization was designed to serve the needs of those with intellectual and developmental disabilities and their families. Select your state's chapter from the website, and then look for your local chapter to see if children services are offered.
2. For medically fragile children, consider contacting a nursing agency to provide in-home care. A few options are mentioned earlier in the chapter.
3. Contemplate utilizing respite care services on occasion for a mental and physical break from caregiving. See list of resources at the end of the book.

Relevant Reading

1. Campbell-Barr, Elyssa. *Choosing Childcare: Nurseries, Registered Childminders, Nannies, Au Pairs, and Family.* Tonbridge: Cross Publishing Services, 2016.
2. Hill, Janelle and Don Philpott. *Special Needs Families in the Military.* Lanham: Government Institutes, 2011.
3. Kelbrat, Tony. *World Au Pair-Nanny-Childcare-Governess-Babysitting-Daycare Guide.* Nova Scotia: Tony Kelbrat, 2015.

CHAPTER 7

Post-traumatic Growth and Your Future

Have you ever heard of post-traumatic growth (PTG)? I was only familiar with post-traumatic stress disorder (PTSD). I discovered PTG while reading an online magazine that advertises wheelchairs and accessories. The article was about several people and their lives prior to an accident and afterward, when they were bound to wheelchairs. I began reading this story and became emotional. Tears rolled down my cheeks because the people profiled were putting words to how my life had been unfolding. The author said, "This is a story that explores one of those ways—an academic-born theory called 'Posttraumatic Growth,' the seemingly outrageous but surprisingly commonsensical idea that certain forms of trauma can help usher in—alongside the pain, sadness, depression and cynicism—positive transformations of one kind or another."[1]

That was it! I knew subconsciously what was manifesting in my life, but this article made it real for me. For Wayne and me, life had been very different before Wyatt was born, and now we were trying to figure out how to live again, and it was difficult. The people in the article were saying that they missed what they once were, but with their new configurations of life, they had become better people. I wanted to shout because I was so excited to learn I wasn't alone in my thinking.

According to Lawrence G. Calhoun and Richard G. Tedeschi, pioneers in the study of post-traumatic growth, "[I]ndividuals can be changed, sometimes in radically good ways, by their struggle with trauma."[2]

---

1 Rucker, Allen. "The Good Side of Trauma." *New Mobility*. August 2010. Retrieved from http://www.newmobility.com/

2 Lawrence G. Calhoun and Richard G. Tedeschi, *Handbook of Posttraumatic Growth* (Mahwah, NJ: Lawrence Erlbaum Associates), ix.

Robin's Recommendations

Having a special-needs child is your traumatic event. By figuring out how to live life purposefully and happily is a huge victory and can be seen as PTG. Since PTG is a broad idea, Calhoun and Tedeschi created five categories of growth I'd like to refer to as SNARP:

Spiritual change
New possibilities
Appreciation of life
Relating to others
Personal strength

With regard to spiritual change, some people gain faith while others lose it. It really depends on where you were with spirituality before the trauma happened. Wayne and I lost faith in God for a while after Wyatt's birth. Theoretically, we both knew we weren't exempt from suffering, but we never imagined that life would be so cruel, and our suffering would come through Wyatt's entry into the world. Neither of us could see God's presence in the situation until years later, after experiencing PTG. We felt angry and abandoned by a God we had actively served. It wasn't until after we ruminated on the situation for a while that one of us recognized what God had done for us in the delivery room. We used to roll the tape in our heads over and over again, saying that God should have inserted His will when Wyatt was delivered and allowed him to breathe right away. After experiencing an epiphany about two years after Wyatt's birth, we instead saw that God had inserted His will and allowed Wyatt's life to be ultimately saved through the pediatrician who had worked on him.

If your child suffers from a diagnosis you believe could have been prevented, it is natural to run that scenario over and over in your head, hoping for the option to reset the clock and have your child placed on his or her rightful path in life. Sometimes parents never get off of this dead-end road. It's not a pleasant place to be, and it brings nothing redeeming into your life. What I can guarantee is that you will be engulfed by lots of anger and resentment unless you actively change your thought process. Since we've been there and done that, I recommend deliberately viewing your situation differently, but this will only come in time.

Wayne and I have redefined happiness for ourselves. Since we were forced to redesign our lives around our new existence with Wyatt, we also discovered we could no longer define *happy* according to how the typically developing world interprets the term. Happy for us means that Wyatt stays consistently healthy for months at a time. Happy also means finding a babysitter who doesn't mind tube feeding and can watch Wyatt for a few hours, so Wayne and I can have fun together as a couple. We also feel very happy when we can develop and maintain great synergy with Wyatt's health-care team. Happiness cocoons us like a cloud when we hang out and do fun things with other special-needs families. We also can stay in our happy place when insurance is covering what we need, when supplies are delivered on time, when equipment continues to work properly, and when enough money is flowing in to cover medical expenses. Of course we experience happy in traditional ways, but we are often blocked from enjoying common experiences of happiness when the things mentioned above become inconsistent.

It's taken me a while to arrive at this thought, but I now savor being different. Our circumstances have forced Wayne and me to reevaluate life and find deeper meaning for our existence. The way we choose to live now is more meaningful than before. We take nothing for granted and try to seize every opportunity (within reason). I feel profoundly blessed that I am able to view life at a level I was previously unable to see or appreciate.

Folks who experience PTG often report a higher level of engagement with life or new possibilities. Calhoun and Tedeschi report that this could manifest through finding new areas of interest, getting involved in new activities, or forging a new career in an area that was never on your radar prior to the trauma. Wayne and I have found deep interests in the study of trauma, how we can rewire ourselves successfully to live happy lives (just differently than before), and being vocal advocates for the special-needs community. Although my husband is a therapist and has dealt with trauma in his office for years, it now has a different meaning to him. Neither of us ever would have imagined wanting to specialize in this area, but our personal trauma has intensified our interest.

I first wanted to learn about trauma to help myself through the process, but then it dawned on me shortly after embarking on this self-educating journey that so many more people could benefit from knowing this information, too. Whatever new possibilities emerge in your life, don't keep them to yourself. Our community has enough land mines to navigate; please help our fellow moms and dads out by sharing your newly found knowledge. You can do this via a personal blog, community groups, your own circle of special-needs families, creating a speaking circuit, or writing your own book.

Calhoun and Tedeschi's third approach to PTG involves an appreciation of life. Those who have been to the brink tend to celebrate life regardless of its current configuration. Often the lives of special-needs parents are changed dramatically from what they were before the traumatic event. Since it takes so much physical, emotional, and sometimes spiritual investment to keep afloat, we often notice that we've grown tremendously as individuals and as couples. Calhoun and Tedeschi noted that people who experience PTG report richer and fuller lives after experiencing trauma. Some folks within this group also report that they would not undo the traumatic event and return to their previous lives because of all of the positive growth they have experienced.

I fall squarely into this category. Although I would love to see Wyatt walk, run, eat with his mouth, hear unaided, and talk, I wouldn't hit the "reset" button because of the tremendous growth Wayne and I have experienced. Our lives are on completely different tracks, and we love who we have become. I don't want to give the impression that hard times don't make our thoughts wander to what life would be like without Wyatt's disability, but the gift our son has given us is the ability to look beyond the physical. Our lives have become enriched by the absence of what the world has deemed important. We have been given a unique and powerful sight and insight that is invaluable.

The fourth approach to PTG is relating to others. Calhoun and Tedeschi report that people tend to have greater connections with others who have experienced similar tragedies. You may find yourself gravitating to other special-needs families because they get your situation without any explanation. You will find comfort and sanctuary with others who belong to our community, and much learning will happen at so many levels for all parties involved.

On the flip side, experiencing trauma sobers you up to the harsh reality that some important folks in your life just weren't there during your greatest time of need. It ultimately doesn't matter why they weren't there; what matters is that you might have been forced to navigate a very difficult situation with little or no support. This is a trauma within itself and can take some time to mend from emotionally. Wayne and I had to take a hard look at our relationships with others to determine if they were fruitful enough to maintain. Since we have less time to deal with nonsense now, we have had to change the dynamics of some relationships and end others. It's your life, and you have the right to define it in a way that fits conveniently into your family-life rhythm.

The last approach to PTG is personal strength. Being on this path sets you up, if you're open to it, for a total transformation. When life blows hurricane-strength winds in your direction, learn to configure yourself in a way that will withstand it and not leave you uprooted. Our lives may look different and unappealing to others outside of our community, but our experiences can be very fulfilling and rewarding.

Reject any pity you or your child might receive. In my opinion, the level of support from family and friends will determine the amount of personal strength you develop. It is a wonderful thing if you have a great network and lots of emotional support, but if you don't, you end up becoming Hercules in your own right. You have to figure everything out on your own and walk an unfamiliar path with very little to no emotional encouragement. This is a tough place to be in, but it is doable. Wayne and I had some support but surprisingly not from as many people as we had hoped. It was very emotionally hurtful to me that some folks weren't willing to be active in our lives due to not knowing what to do or say, but we lived and thrived in spite of their absence. During this process, you learn a lot of truth about people, whether you want to know it or not. Relationships can be restored through honest and frank conversations about what you need and what is missing from them, or you can choose to keep living strongly without them. It's your life and totally up to you if time permits to nurture a relationship that might no longer be beneficial.

I'm not sure where you are on your journey, but I know you have had a plethora of experiences that are similar to ours. If you're in the NICU, please don't let the medical professionals discourage you. What they say right now doesn't define how the rest of your life will shape up. Upon Wyatt's discharge from the NICU, the medical team told us he would never hit any milestones. We were devastated by that news, but it didn't define us or how we ultimately decided to live our lives. Wyatt has not hit traditional milestones such as crawling, walking, or talking, but he is thriving and happy.

If you find yourself frustrated by family and friends because they don't seem to understand your situation or your child's disability, remember that it isn't your job to help them understand. Your time is limited, so spend it wisely. Those who genuinely want to help will proactively get involved. Also remember that success and lifelong happiness can be achieved with a special-needs child; they are just defined differently. We know this road is hard, but it is rewarding. We wish you much success on your journey and hope to meet you one day. It is an honor and privilege to be on this journey and share our insight and experiences with you. Thank you for reading!

Rapid Review

1. Embrace post-traumatic growth. Turn your trauma into significant growth opportunities.
2. Look at your current life configuration differently, and stop comparing it to families with typically developing children.
3. Redefine what makes you happy. Meaningful happiness can include the most mundane things like supplies being delivered on time. When critical items aren't there when you need them, life isn't so happy.

Relevant Reading

1. Haas, Michael. *Bouncing Forward: Transforming Bad Breaks into Breakthroughs.* New York: Enliven, 2015.
2. Rendon, Jim. *Upside: The New Science of Post-Traumatic Growth.* New York: Touchstone, 2016.
3. Seligman, Martin E.P. *Flourish: A Visionary New Understanding of Happiness and Well-being.* New York: Free Press, 2012.

Works Cited

Lawrence G. Calhoun and Richard G. Tedeschi, *Handbook of Posttraumatic Growth* (Mahwah, NJ: Lawrence Erlbaum Associates), ix.

Rucker, Allen. "The Good Side of Trauma." *New Mobility*. August 2010. Retrieved from http://www.newmobility.com.

Further Reading

Chapter 1

1. Byrne, Rhonda. *The Secret*. New York: Atria Books, Oregon: Beyond Words Publishing, 2006.
2. Cousins, Norman. *Head First: The Biology of Hope and Healing Power of the Human Spirit*. New York: Penguin Books, 1990.
3. Singer, Jonathan. *The Special Needs Parent Handbook, Critical Strategies and Practical Advice to Help You Survive and Thrive*. New Jersey: Clinton+Valley Publishing, 2012.

Chapter 2

1. Coleman, Avis. *SPECIAL NEEDS: Special Families*. IN: AuthorHouse, 2014.
2. Cooper, Contessa Louise. *Mad at the World: How to Move On and Find Peace When You're A Special Needs Parent*. MD: Contessa Louise, 2015.
3. Hernandez, Geri. *Medically Fragile Training Manual*. OK: Tate Publishing & Enterprises, LLC, 2010.

Chapter 3

1. Bradley, Lorna. Special Needs Parenting: From Coping to Thriving. MN: Huff Publishing Associates, 2015.
2. Kimpton, Diana. *A Special Child in the Family: Living with your sick or disabled child*. London: Sheldon Press, 2011.
3. Philo, Jolene. *Different Dream Parenting: A Practical Guide to Raising a Child with Special Needs*. MI: Discovery House Publishers, 2011.

Chapter 4

1. Lavin, Judith Loseff. *Special Kids Need Special Parents: A Resource for Parents of Children with Special Needs.* New York: Berkley, 2001.
2. Vujicic, Boris. *Raising the Perfectly Imperfect Child: Facing the Challenges with Strength, Courage, and Hope.* Colorado: WaterBrook, 2017.
3. Wells, Nora. *Paying the Bills: Tips for Families on Financing Health Care for Children with Special Needs.* Boston: New England SERVE, 1999.

Chapter 5

1. Crawford, Merle J. and Barbara Weber. *Early Intervention Every Day!: Embedding Activities in Daily Routines for Young Children and Their Families.* Baltimore: Brookes Publishing, 2013.
2. Kaufman, Sandra and Robert Edgerton. *Retarded Isn't Stupid, Mom!* Baltimore: Brookes Publishing, 1999.
3. Keilty, Bonnie. *The Early Intervention Guidebook for Families and Professionals: Partnering for Success.* New York: Teachers College Press, 2016.

Chapter 6

1. Campbell-Barr, Elyssa. *Choosing Childcare: Nurseries, Registered Childminders, Nannies, Au Pairs, and Family.* Tonbridge: Cross Publishing Services, 2016.
2. Hill, Janelle and Don Philpott. *Special Needs Families in the Military.* Lanham: Government Institutes, 2011.
3. Kelbrat, Tony. *World Au Pair-Nanny-Childcare-Governess-Babysitting-Daycare Guide.* Nova Scotia: Tony Kelbrat, 2015.

Chapter 7

1. Haas, Michael. *Bouncing Forward: Transforming Bad Breaks into Breakthroughs.* New York: Enliven, 2015.
2. Rendon, Jim. *Upside: The New Science of Post-Traumatic Growth.* New York: Touchstone, 2016.
3. Seligman, Martin E.P. *Flourish: A Visionary New Understanding of Happiness and Well-being.* New York: Free Press, 2012.

Resources

Advocacy

National Coalition for Assistive and Rehab Technology: www.ncart.us

National Registry of Rehabilitation Technology Suppliers: www.nrrts.org

Special education law and advocacy for children with disabilities: www.wrightslaw.com

Childcare

Care.com (global childcare organization): www.care.com/special-needs

Easter Seals (childcare services): www.easterseals.com

Jill's House (DC metro area): jillshouse.org

Saint Joseph's House (DC metro area): www.saintjosephshouse.net

The Arc: www.thearc.org

The Arc Montgomery County (Maryland): thearcmontgomerycounty.org

Equipment

AMS Vans, Inc. (grants for wheelchair-accessible vans for people with cerebral palsy): www.amsvans.com/financing-handicap-vans

Equipment Connections for Children, Inc.: www.equipforchildren.org

Make-A-Wish Foundation (for equipment requests in lieu of trips): www.wish.org

Family

"50 Great Websites for Parents of Children with Special Needs": www.masters-in-special-education.com/50-great-websites-for-parents-of-children-with-special-needs

Abilitytree.org: abilitytree.org

ExpatArrivals (living abroad with a special-needs child): www.expatarrivals.com/article/living-abroad-with-a-special-needs-child

First Signs, Inc. (a national nonprofit organization dedicated to educating parents and professionals about the early warning signs of autism and related disorders): www.firstsigns.org

Friendshipcircle.org (Israel): www.friendshipcircle.org/blog

Joni and Friends International Disability Center: www.joniandfriends.org

Joyful Journey Mom: joyfuljourneymom.com

National Center on Deaf-Blindness: nationaldb.org/families

National Responsible Fatherhood Clearinghouse (dads' supportive communities): www.fatherhood.gov/for-dads/connect-with-programs

PhDinSpecialEducation.com (extensive list of resources and supportive communities): phdinspecialeducation.com/special-needs-parenting-handbook

Support for Families of Children with Disabilities (parent-to-parent resources, including a site for dads with special-needs children): www.supportforfamilies.org/internetguide/parents.html

The Center for Parent Information and Resources (serves as a central resource of information and products for families of children with disabilities): www.parentcenterhub.org

Funding

Act Today (grants for autistic children): www.act-today.org

Danielle's Foundation (grants for children with cerebral palsy and brain injuries): www.daniellesfoundation.org

eSpecialNeeds.com (funding resources for special-needs and adaptive equipment): www.especialneeds.com/funding-resources-special-needs-adaptive-equipment.html

Federal government (disability benefits): www.disability.gov

Lollipop Kids Foundation: www.lollipopkidsfoundation.org

Low Intensity Support Services (LISS; Maryland residents only): dda.dhmh.maryland.gov

My Turn (Maryland residents only): www.montgomerycountymd.gov (search "My Turn Program")

United Health Care Children's Foundation (medical grants): www.uhccf.org

Services

ARCH National Respite Network: archrespite.org/respitelocator

AutismOntario (Canada): www.autismontario.com

BrightStar Care (pediatric nursing and babysitting): www.brightstarcare.com

Care.com (serves Australia, Austria, Belgium, Canada, Denmark, Finland, France, Germany, Ireland, Netherlands, Spain, Sweden, Switzerland, United Kingdom, and the United States): www.care.com/SpecialNeeds

Care.com (ten additional organizations that assist with resources and funding): www.care.com/a/10-helpful-special-needs-organizations-1210250634

Cerebralpalsy.org: cerebralpalsy.org

Charity Village (Canada): charityvillage.com/directories/organizations-a-h/disabilities.aspx

Childsafe.com (special needs resource links to local and national organizations): childsafe.com/t_special_needs_resources.php

Christopher and Dana Reeve Foundation (extensive list of resources):

www.christopherreeve.org

Continuum Pediatric Nursing: www.Continuum-Nursing.com

Disabled People's Association Singapore: www.dpa.org.sg

Eurordis Rare Diseases Europe: www.eurordis.org/specialised-social-services

Federal government (disability benefits): www.disability.gov/home/i_want_to/disability_benefits

Florence (Japan): byojihoiku.florence.or.jp

Friendshipcircle.org (multiple special-needs organizations in Israel): www.friendshipcircle.org/blog

Government of South Australia: www.sa.gov.au

Global Campaign for Education: www.campaignforeducation.org

Interim Healthcare (pediatric nursing): www.interimhealthcare.com

Karen for Kids (pediatric nursing for the DC metro area): www.karenforkids.com

KidsHealth: kidshealth.org/en/parents/respite-care.html#

LovethatMax.com (twenty-two free things, services, and grants for kids with special needs): www.lovethatmax.com/2015/04/ free-things-for-kids-with-special-needs.html

Maxim Home Care: www.maximhomecare.com

MetroKids:www.metrokids.com/MetroKids/January-2010/Respite-You-Deserve-a-Break-Today

National Association of the Deaf & Hard of Hearing (click on the "Parents" link to get information pertaining to children): nad.org

National Autism Resources: www.nationalautismresources.com

National Down Syndrome Society: www.ndss.org/Down-Syndrome

National Military Family Association- www.militaryfamily.org

One Place for Special Needs (practical resources to help your children now): www.oneplaceforspecialneeds.com

PROaupair: proaupair.com

Rainbowkids.co.za (Kidstart Early Intervention Centre located in Cape Town, South Africa): www.rainbowkids.co.za

Right to Educate Project (South Africa): www.right-to-education.org/blog

Sittercity: www.sittercity.com

Special education terminology glossary: www.inclusivechildcare.org/inclusion_glossary.cfm

Saint Michael's House (Ireland): www.smh.ie

State Department (resources on special needs while living abroad): www.state.gov/m/a/os/c18630.htm

Support and Resources for Parents and Teachers: www.specialeducationguide.com

The Early Intervention Program for Infants and Toddlers with Disabilities (Part C of IDEA): ectacenter.org/families.asp

The National Children's Cancer Society (special education information by state): www.thenccs.org

The YMCA: www.ymca.org

United Cerebral Palsy: ucp.org

Zero to Three (early development): www.zerotothree.org

Therapy

American Psychological Association: www.apa.org

Association of Black Psychologists: www.abpsi.org

Couples therapy: www.gettingtheloveyouwant.com

Family Life (hosts "weekend to remember" getaways in major cities throughout the year): www.familylife.com

Ginny Paleg (physical therapist located in the DC metro area, but conducts video assessments for children not in the area): www.ginnypaleg.com

About the Author

Robin Williams Evans is originally from the Los Angeles, California, area. She attended California State University Long Beach, where she majored in business administration with a concentration in marketing. In 1998, Robin heard a call from God to enter into ministry. She received her master's in divinity from Howard University School of Divinity in 2004 and was ordained in 2010. Robin served as an associate minister for twelve years at Riverside Baptist Church of Southwest Washington, DC, where Reverend Dr. Michael Bledsoe is the pastor.

Robin is the founder and director of A Pastor's Place (www.apastorsplace.org), a not-for-profit organization that specializes in spiritual, emotional, and physical health and wellness for clergy and church congregations and special-needs advocacy.

She is a firm believer in post-traumatic growth and its tremendous ability to take crises and turn them into firm foundations that transform people into their best selves. Robin is a wife and the mother of a severely special-needs son.

Made in the USA
Middletown, DE
15 July 2017